Master Your Time

A Quick Guide to Time Management for Beginners

Baxter Prescott

<u>Table of Contents:</u>

Introduction

Time is a precious resource. It is the one thing that we all have in common, and yet it is also the one thing that we can never get back. In today's fast-paced world, it is more important than ever to learn how to manage our time effectively.

This book is designed to help you do just that. It will teach you the essential skills and strategies you need to master your time and achieve your goals.

In the chapters that follow, you will learn:

- Why time management is important
- How to set goals and priorities
- How to plan and schedule your time
- How to delegate effectively
- How to overcome procrastination
- How to manage your energy

By following the advice in this book, you will be well on your way to becoming a master of your time. You will be able to achieve more, reduce stress, and live a more fulfilling life.

Here are some of the benefits of effective time management:

- You will be more productive and get more done.
- You will reduce stress and feel more in control of your life.
- You will have more time for the things that are important to you.
- You will be more successful in your personal and professional life.

If you are ready to take control of your time and improve your life, then this book is for you.

Chapter 1: Why Time Management Matters

Time management is the process of planning, organizing, and executing tasks in order to achieve goals. It is a skill that can be learned and improved with practice.

There are many benefits to effective time management. When you manage your time well, you can:

- **Get more done**
- **Reduce stress**
- **Improve your productivity**
- **Achieve your goals**

If you are feeling overwhelmed by your workload or if you are not achieving your goals, then time management may be the answer for you.

Here are some of the specific benefits of effective time management:

- **Increased productivity:** When you manage your time well, you are able to focus on the most important tasks and get them done efficiently. This can lead to increased productivity and results.

- **Reduced stress:** When you feel like you are in control of your time, you are less likely to feel stressed. This can lead to improved mental and physical health.
- **Improved focus:** When you have a plan and a schedule, you are less likely to be distracted by unimportant tasks. This can lead to improved focus and concentration.
- **Achieved goals:** When you manage your time effectively, you are more likely to achieve your goals. This can lead to a sense of accomplishment and satisfaction.

In addition to these general benefits, effective time management can also help you:

- **Improve your relationships:** When you have more time for the things that are important to you, you are more likely to have strong relationships with your loved ones.
- **Be more prepared:** When you plan and schedule your time, you are less likely to be caught off guard by unexpected events.
- **Be more flexible:** When you have a good understanding of your time, you are more likely to be able to adapt to changes.

If you are ready to start improving your time management skills, there are a few things you can do.

- **Set goals and priorities:** The first step to effective time management is to set goals and priorities. What are the most important things you want to achieve? Once you know your goals, you can prioritize your tasks accordingly.
- **Plan and schedule your time:** Once you know your goals and priorities, you can start planning and scheduling your time. This will help you stay on track and avoid procrastination.
- **Delegate tasks:** Don't be afraid to delegate tasks to others. This will free up your time so you can focus on the most important things.
- **Avoid distractions:** Distractions can be a major time-waster. When you are working on a task, try to eliminate distractions as much as possible.
- **Take breaks:** It is important to take breaks throughout the day to avoid burnout. Get up and move around, or take a few minutes to relax and clear your head.

By following these tips, you can learn how to manage your time effectively and achieve your goals.

Here are some additional tips for effective time management:

- **Be realistic about your time constraints.** Don't try to do too much in too little time.
- **Be flexible and adaptable.** Things don't always go according to plan, so be prepared to make changes as needed.
- **Don't be afraid to say no.** It's okay to turn down requests that will take up too much of your time.
- **Learn to say no to yourself.** It's easy to get caught up in distractions, so learn to focus on the task at hand.

Time management is a skill that takes time and practice to develop. By following the tips in this chapter, you can start improving your time management skills today.

Here are some additional resources that you may find helpful:

- **Books:** The 7 Habits of Highly Effective People by Stephen R. Covey, Getting Things Done by David Allen, The Power of Now by Eckhart Tolle
- **Websites:** Time Management Ninja, Lifehack, The Productivity Project
- **Apps:** Any.do, Wunderlist, ToDoist

Chapter 2: Set Goals and Priorities

Goals and priorities are the foundation of effective time management. When you know what you want to achieve and what is most important to you, you can focus your time and energy on the things that will make the biggest difference.

In this chapter, we will discuss the importance of setting goals and priorities, and we will provide tips for doing so effectively.

Why are goals and priorities important?

- **Goals give you direction.** When you know what you want to achieve, you can make decisions about how to allocate your time and resources.
- **Priorities help you focus.** Not all tasks are created equal. By prioritizing your tasks, you can focus on the most important ones and avoid wasting time on unimportant tasks.
- **Goals and priorities can help you stay motivated.** When you have something to work towards, it is easier to stay motivated and avoid procrastination.

How to set goals

- **Make sure your goals are specific, measurable, achievable, relevant, and time-bound.** This will help you stay focused and on track.
- **Write down your goals.** This will help you keep them top of mind.
- **Break down your goals into smaller, more manageable tasks.** This will make them seem less daunting and more achievable.

How to prioritize tasks

- **Consider the importance of each task.** Which tasks are essential to achieving your goals?
- **Consider the urgency of each task.** Which tasks need to be done right away?
- **Consider your resources.** Do you have the time, energy, and skills to complete each task?

How to create a schedule

- **Be realistic about your time constraints.** Don't try to do too much in too little time.
- **Leave some flexibility in your schedule for unexpected events.**
- Be willing to adjust your schedule as needed.

Additional tips for setting goals and priorities

- **Get feedback from others.** Ask friends, family, or colleagues for their input on your goals and priorities.
- **Set deadlines for yourself.** Deadlines can help you stay motivated and on track.
- **Reward yourself for your accomplishments.** This will help you stay motivated and keep moving forward.

Conclusion

Setting goals and priorities is an essential part of effective time management. By following the tips in this chapter, you can develop a plan for achieving your goals and living a more fulfilling life.

Here are some additional thoughts on setting goals and priorities:

- **Goals should be ambitious but achievable.** If your goals are too easy, you will not be motivated to achieve them. If your goals are too difficult, you will be discouraged and give up.
- **It is important to review your goals and priorities regularly.** As your life changes, your goals and priorities may need to change as well.
- **There is no one right way to set goals and priorities.** Experiment with different methods until you find one that works for you.

Chapter 3: Plan and Schedule Your Time

Planning and scheduling your time is essential for effective time management. When you have a plan, you are more likely to stay on track and avoid procrastination.

In this chapter, we will discuss the importance of planning and scheduling your time, and we will provide tips for doing so effectively.

Why is planning and scheduling important?

- **It helps you stay on track.** When you have a plan, you know what you need to do and when you need to do it. This can help you avoid getting sidetracked or overwhelmed.
- **It helps you avoid procrastination.** When you have a plan, you are less likely to put off tasks until the last minute.
- **It can help you be more productive.** When you know what you need to do and when you need to do it, you can focus your time and energy on the most important tasks.

How to plan your time

- **Start by setting goals and priorities.** Once you know what you want to achieve, you can start to plan how you will achieve it.
- **Break down your goals into smaller, more manageable tasks.** This will make it easier to develop a plan.
- **Estimate how long each task will take.** This will help you create a realistic schedule.
- **Leave some flexibility in your schedule.** Unexpected events can happen, so it is important to have some wiggle room.

How to schedule your time

- **Start by listing all of your tasks.** This includes both work and personal tasks.
- **Prioritize your tasks.** Focus on the most important tasks first.
- **Schedule your tasks in a logical order.** This will help you stay on track.
- **Block out time for each task.** This will help you stay focused.
- **Be flexible.** Things don't always go according to plan, so be prepared to adjust your schedule as needed.

Additional tips for planning and scheduling your time

- **Use a time management tool or app.** There are many different tools and apps available to help you plan and schedule your time.
- **Delegate tasks.** Don't be afraid to delegate tasks to others. This will free up your time so you can focus on the most important things.
- **Say no.** It's okay to say no to requests that will take up too much of your time.
- **Take breaks.** It is important to take breaks throughout the day to avoid burnout.

Conclusion

Planning and scheduling your time is an essential part of effective time management. By following the tips in this chapter, you can develop a plan for achieving your goals and living a more fulfilling life.

Here are some additional thoughts on planning and scheduling your time:

- **Your plan should be flexible.** Things don't always go according to plan, so be prepared to adjust your schedule as needed.
- **It is important to review your plan regularly.** As your life changes, your plan may need to change as well.
- **There is no one right way to plan and schedule your time.** Experiment with different methods until you find one that works for you.

Chapter 4: Delegate Effectively

Delegation is the process of assigning tasks or responsibilities to others. It can be a valuable time management tool, as it can free up your time so you can focus on the most important tasks.

In this chapter, we will discuss the importance of delegation, how to delegate effectively, and the benefits of delegation.

Why is delegation important?

- **It can free up your time.** When you delegate tasks to others, you can focus on the tasks that are most important to you.
- **It can improve your productivity.** When you delegate tasks to others, you can get more done in less time.
- **It can help you develop your team.** Delegation can be a great way to develop the skills and abilities of your team members.
- **It can improve your relationships.** When you delegate tasks to others, you are showing them that you trust them and value their contributions.

How to delegate effectively

- **Choose the right tasks to delegate.** Not all tasks are appropriate for delegation. Choose tasks that are routine, non-critical, and that can be done by someone else.
- **Choose the right people to delegate to.** Make sure that the people you delegate to have the skills, knowledge, and authority to complete the tasks.
- **Provide clear instructions.** When you delegate a task, be sure to provide clear instructions so that the person you are delegating to knows what is expected of them.
- **Set deadlines.** Deadlines can help keep the person you are delegating to on track.
- **Follow up.** Check in with the person you are delegating to to see how they are doing and to provide any additional support they may need.

Benefits of delegation

- **Increased productivity:** Delegation can free up your time so you can focus on the tasks that are most important to you. This can lead to increased productivity and results.
- **Reduced stress:** When you delegate tasks, you are no longer responsible for completing them. This can help reduce stress and improve your overall well-being.

- **Improved relationships:** Delegation can show your team members that you trust them and value their contributions. This can lead to improved relationships and collaboration.

Conclusion

Delegation is a valuable time management tool that can help you free up your time, improve your productivity, and reduce stress. By following the tips in this chapter, you can learn how to delegate effectively and reap the benefits of delegation.

Here are some additional thoughts on delegation:

- **Don't be afraid to delegate tasks to others.** Even if you think you can do the task better yourself, it may be worth it to delegate it to someone else in order to free up your time.
- **Be willing to train the people you delegate to.** If the person you are delegating to does not have the skills or knowledge to complete the task, be willing to train them.
- **Be patient.** It may take some time for the person you are delegating to to learn how to complete the task effectively.

Chapter 5: Overcome Procrastination

Procrastination is the act of delaying or postponing a task or set of tasks. It is a common problem that can have a negative impact on our productivity, our relationships, and our overall well-being.

In this chapter, we will discuss the causes of procrastination, the negative consequences of procrastination, and how to overcome procrastination.

Causes of procrastination

There are many different causes of procrastination. Some of the most common causes include:

- **Fear of failure:** We may procrastinate on a task because we are afraid of failing.
- **Perfectionism:** We may procrastinate on a task because we want to do it perfectly.
- **Lack of motivation:** We may procrastinate on a task because we are not motivated to do it.
- **Distractions:** We may procrastinate on a task because we are easily distracted.
- **Laziness:** We may procrastinate on a task because we are simply lazy.

Negative consequences of procrastination

Procrastination can have a number of negative consequences, including:

- **Reduced productivity:** Procrastination can lead to missed deadlines, poor quality work, and increased stress.
- **Damaged relationships:** Procrastination can strain our relationships with our colleagues, our family, and our friends.
- **Reduced self-esteem:** Procrastination can lead to feelings of guilt, shame, and low self-esteem.
- **Increased anxiety and depression:** Procrastination can lead to increased anxiety and depression.

How to overcome procrastination

There are a number of things we can do to overcome procrastination, including:

- **Identify the underlying causes of your procrastination.** Once you know why you procrastinate, you can start to develop strategies to overcome it.
- **Break down large tasks into smaller, more manageable tasks.** This will make the task seem less daunting and more achievable.

- **Set deadlines for yourself.** Deadlines can help you stay motivated and on track.
- **Eliminate distractions.** When you are working on a task, find a quiet place where you will not be interrupted.
- **Reward yourself for completing tasks.** This will help you stay motivated and on track.
- **Talk to someone you trust about your procrastination.** Talking about your procrastination can help you identify the underlying causes and develop a plan to overcome it.
- **Join a procrastination support group.** There are many online and in-person support groups available for people who struggle with procrastination.
- **Seek professional help.** If your procrastination is severe, you may need to seek professional help from a therapist or counselor.

Conclusion

Procrastination is a common problem that can have a negative impact on our lives. By following the tips in this chapter, we can overcome procrastination and improve our productivity, our relationships, and our overall well-being.

Here are some additional thoughts on overcoming procrastination:

- **Procrastination is a habit.** It takes time and effort to break any habit, including procrastination.
- **Be patient with yourself.** Don't expect to overcome procrastination overnight.
- **Don't give up.** With time and effort, you can overcome procrastination and achieve your goals.

Here are some additional resources that you may find helpful:

- **Books:** The Procrastination Cure by Timothy Pychyl, The Now Habit by Neil Fiore, The Power of Habit by Charles Duhigg
- **Websites:** Procrastination.org, The Procrastination Project, The Productivityist
- **Apps:** Procrastination Timer, Focus Booster, Forest

Chapter 6: Manage Your Energy

Energy is just as important as time when it comes to productivity. When we are well-rested and energized, we are better able to focus, concentrate, and get things done.

In this chapter, we will discuss the importance of managing your energy, how to do it effectively, and the benefits of energy management.

Why is energy management important?

- **It can help you be more productive.** When you are well-rested and energized, you are better able to focus, concentrate, and get things done.
- **It can help you avoid burnout.** Burnout is a state of physical, emotional, and mental exhaustion. It can be caused by chronic stress and overwork. By managing your energy, you can reduce your risk of burnout.
- **It can improve your overall health and well-being.** When you are well-rested and energized, you are better able to take care of yourself physically and mentally.

How to manage your energy effectively

- **Get enough sleep.** Most adults need 7-8 hours of sleep per night.
- **Eat a healthy diet.** Eating healthy foods can give you the energy you need to get through the day.
- **Exercise regularly.** Exercise is a great way to boost your energy levels.
- **Take breaks throughout the day.** Get up and move around every 20-30 minutes to avoid getting too tired.
- **Do things that you enjoy.** When you do things that you enjoy, you are more likely to feel energized.
- **Avoid caffeine and alcohol.** Caffeine and alcohol can disrupt your sleep, which can lead to fatigue.
- **Manage stress.** Stress can drain your energy levels. Find healthy ways to manage stress, such as exercise, relaxation techniques, or spending time with loved ones.

Benefits of energy management

- **Increased productivity:** When you are well-rested and energized, you are better able to focus, concentrate, and get things done.
- **Reduced stress:** When you are well-rested and energized, you are better able to manage stress.

- **Improved health:** When you are well-rested and energized, you are better able to take care of yourself physically and mentally.
- **Increased happiness:** When you are well-rested and energized, you are more likely to feel happy and positive.

Conclusion

Energy management is an important part of overall health and well-being. By following the tips in this chapter, you can learn how to manage your energy effectively and reap the benefits of energy management.

Here are some additional thoughts on energy management:

- **It is important to find what works best for you.** There is no one-size-fits-all approach to energy management. Experiment with different techniques and find what helps you feel your best.
- **Don't be afraid to ask for help.** If you are struggling to manage your energy, talk to a doctor or therapist. They can help you develop a plan that works for you.

Conclusion

Time management is a skill that can be learned and improved with practice. By following the tips in this book, you can learn how to better manage your time, achieve your goals, and live a more fulfilling life.

Here are some key takeaways from this book:

- **Set goals and priorities.** When you know what you want to achieve, you can focus your time and energy on the most important tasks.
- **Plan and schedule your time.** This will help you stay on track and avoid procrastination.
- **Delegate tasks effectively.** This will free up your time so you can focus on the most important tasks.
- **Overcome procrastination.** This can be a difficult habit to break, but there are a number of things you can do to make it easier.
- **Manage your energy.** When you are well-rested and energized, you are better able to focus, concentrate, and get things done.

Remember, time management is a journey, not a destination. There will be ups and downs along the way, but by following the tips in this book, you can learn to manage your time more effectively and achieve your goals.

Here are some additional thoughts on time management:

- **Time management is not about being perfect.** It is about making the most of the time you have.
- **It is important to be flexible.** Things don't always go according to plan, so be prepared to adjust your schedule as needed.
- **Don't be afraid to ask for help.** If you are struggling to manage your time, talk to a friend, family member, or professional.

I hope this book has given you the tools and inspiration you need to improve your time management skills.